Graphic Chillers

WEREWOLF

WRITTEN
AND
ILLUSTRATED BY
JEFF ZORNOW

WEREWOLF

ABOUT WEREWOLVES

Werewolves were believed to exist in prehistoric times. In Greek, Roman, and Norse mythology, werewolves were men who changed into wolves by magic spells or herbs. They were written about by the Greek historian Herodotus and the Roman poet Virgil.

The myths spread to Europe during the Middle Ages. There, French laws expelled werewolves from the country. English, German and Russian peasants also had tales of men turning into wolves.

Today, werewolves can be found in modern fiction. Horror tales are told of men bitten by a werewolf who change against their will at the time of the full moon. They devour animals and people but return to human form during the day. In many stories, a werewolf cannot die, though in the Hollywood versions of the myth it can be killed with a silver bullet.

In 1933, Guy Endore wrote *Werewolf in Paris*, which inspired films such as *The Wolf Man*. More recently, J.K. Rowling included werewolves in the Harry Potter series. R.L. Stine and Stephen Cole have also produced books about the mysterious creature.

THERE IS EVIL IN THIS WORLD.

AND HERE IN THE BEAUTIFUL CARPATHIAN MOUNTAINS, WE, THE INHABITANTS OF THE TOWN OF DREDSAD, ARE NOT SPARED FROM THIS EVIL.

IT CAME TO US LONG AGO, IN THE DARK FORM OF THE UNDEAD... A VAMPIRE NAMED *WANDESSA*.

A PRINCESS OF THE *FOUL NIGHT* WHO DWELLED IN THE RUINED TOWER HIGH ABOVE DREDSAD.

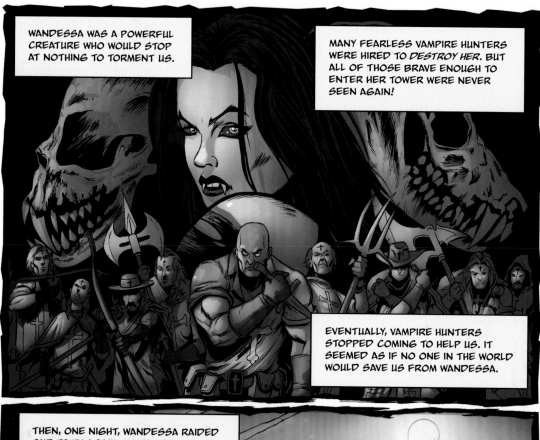

WANDESSA WAS A POWERFUL CREATURE WHO WOULD STOP AT NOTHING TO TORMENT US.

MANY FEARLESS VAMPIRE HUNTERS WERE HIRED TO *DESTROY HER*. BUT ALL OF THOSE BRAVE ENOUGH TO ENTER HER TOWER WERE NEVER SEEN AGAIN!

EVENTUALLY, VAMPIRE HUNTERS STOPPED COMING TO HELP US. IT SEEMED AS IF NO ONE IN THE WORLD WOULD SAVE US FROM WANDESSA.

THEN, ONE NIGHT, WANDESSA RAIDED OUR TOWN AGAIN. MANY PEOPLE WERE *KILLED*, BUT WORSE THAN THAT...

...SHE *STOLE* TWO YOUNG CHILDREN!

THE TOWNS PEOPLE HAD BEEN PUSHED *TOO FAR*! WE DECIDED TO TRY A PLAN THAT WOULD RID OUR HOME OF THIS VAMPIRE'S TORTURE FOR ALL TIME.

THE PLAN WAS *VERY RISKY*, WITH A HIGH CHANCE OF *FAILURE*.

BUT SOMETHING *HAD* TO BE DONE!

THE NEXT AFTERNOON, A HORSE AND CART ARRIVED AT WANDESSA'S RUINED TOWER.

A STRANGER TO OUR TOWN WAS UNLOADED FROM THE CART.

THIS MAN, WHO HAD NO NAME HE COULD REMEMBER, SAID HE COULD DESTROY WANDESSA FOR A SMALL PAYMENT. THIS SOMBRE MAN NEEDED NO *WEAPONS* OR *HOLY ITEMS* TO FIGHT OFF THE VAMPIRE. ALL HE ASKED IS THAT WE *CHAIN HIM* SECURELY TO A TREE.

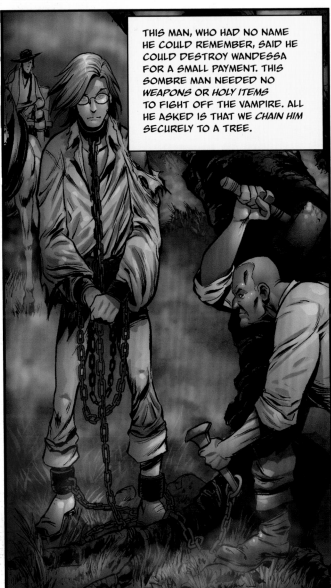

I WAS HIDING IN BUSHES NEARBY – MY NAME IS FATHER BASTA, AND THIS IS WHERE *I* ENTER OUR STORY.

I FELT IT WAS MY *DUTY* TO TAKE A STAND AGAINST THE EVIL THAT WAS *PLAGUING* MY PARISH. EVEN THOUGH IT SEEMED TO REQUIRE MAKING A DEAL WITH THE *DEVIL*.

FOR ONLY I KNEW THE MYSTERIOUS MAN'S *DREADFUL SECRET*.

YOU!

HUH? HUH? WHA- WHAT IS THIS?!

YOU THERE!

WHAT ARE YOU DOING HERE?!

SNORT!

AND I *PRAYED* THAT THIS MAN WOULD HELP ME SAVE THE MISSING CHILDREN.

THIS IS THE HOME OF THE GREAT *WANDESSA THE VAMPIRE!* AND YOU HAVE CAUSED HARM TO HER... ER... *TREE!*

MY FRIEND, IT IS *YOU* WHO SHALL BE *WARNED.* I AM HERE TO *DESTROY* WANDESSA AND ALL THE EVIL THAT SHE BRINGS. I AM CHAINED TO THIS TREE TO HELP ENSURE THAT MY *FURY* DOES NOT WANDER TO THE TOWN OF DREDSAD. GO AND TELL YOUR MISTRESS THAT HER *REIGN OF BLOOD* ENDS TONIGHT.

IT WILL BE HARD TO DO *ANYTHING* WHILE YOU ARE CHAINED TO A TREE!

FOR THIS YOU WILL SUFFER A FATE WORSE THAN *DEATH! BE WARNED!*

EXCEPT GET *YOURSELF* KILLED!

...AND HE'S CHAINED TO A TREE! HE CLAIMS HE IS HERE TO *DESTROY* YOU MY MISTRESS!

I LISTENED TO THE CREATURE CURSE AS HE WENT BACK TO REPORT TO HIS MISTRESS.

INTERESTING... I WONDER WHAT MANNER OF MAN THEY MAY HAVE SENT TO ME...HE SOUNDS LIKE A *FOOL!*

HAVEN'T THOSE PEASANTS LEARNED THERE IS NOT A HUMAN ON THIS EARTH WHO CAN *STOP* ME?

THIS FOOL OF A MAN SHALL BE DEALT WITH AS I LAY IN MY COFFIN AWAITING THE COLD NIGHT!

AND AFTER HIS BONES LAY *BARE* IN THE MOONLIGHT, I SHALL TAKE THESE TWO CHILDREN TO BECOME THE FIRST OF MY CULT. I WILL TURN THEM INTO *VAMPIRES*, ENSLAVED BY BLOOD.

FOR I AM WANDESSA *PRINCESS OF DARKNESS! MISTRESS OF THE DEAD AND DECAYED! AND I COMMAND THEM TO RISE!!*

RISE!! RISE FROM YOUR COLD AND NAMELESS GRAVES! KILL MY ENEMY!

I WAS STUNNED TO SEE ROTTEN SKELETONS *RISE UP* OUT OF THE GROUND. THE HORRID VISION MADE MY HEART SINK.

A'EeEeE!

THE DEAD QUICKLY SWARMED THE MAN. A *SICKENING SIGHT*, THE CREATURES WERE TRYING TO *EAT HIM!*

THEN I NOTICED THE SUN.

IT WAS SINKING BELOW THE HORIZON...

...AND I KNEW WANDESSA WOULD SOON BE OUT!

NOW LET ME SEE THE BONES OF THIS *FOOL* WHO CHAINED HIMSELF TO MY TREE!

EH? WHAT'S THIS?

YOU'RE *STILL* ALIVE!?

YES! I AM CERTAINLY STILL HERE. I SWORE TO DESTROY THE TERROR YOU BRING TO THE PEOPLE OF DREDSAD. I AM AFFLICTED WITH AN *EVIL* THAT IS WITHOUT **CONTROL** OR *LIMIT*. A *CURSE* MORE POWERFUL THAN YOUR DARK DESIRES.

THEN, AS A FULL MOON RISE IN THE SKY, I BECAME WITNESS TO SOME KIND OF BLACK MAGIC.

THE MAN BURIED BENEATH ROTTEN SKELETONS SEEMED TO BE TRANSFORMING!

HE WAS GROWING WIRY HAIR AND LONG CLAWS! IT SEEMED NOT OF THIS EARTH.

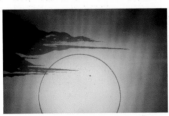

GOOD LORD!

RRRRR

WHA-? HE-HE'S A...

IT WAS AS IF I COULD HEAR THE VAMPIRE IN MY HEAD, MOCKING ME.

HA HA! PLEASE! STEP INTO MY PARLOUR SAID THE SPIDER TO THE FLY!

IT WAS PITCH BLACK AS I STEPPED INSIDE THE TOWER. I COULD HEAR THE SOUNDS OF ANIMALS FIGHTING.

AND AS MY EYES ADJUSTED TO THE DARK I WAS HORRIFIED BY WHAT I SAW.

A GIANT MONSTER SPIDER! THE WEREWOLF WAS STANDING HIS GROUND BATTLING THE HUGE ARACHNID.

WITH AN AWESOME DISPLAY OF STRENGTH, THE WEREWOLF THREW THE GIANT SPIDER INTO A CRUMBLED WELL!

GRAH!

AND WASTED NO TIME IN ATTACKING THE SPIDER'S SOFT UNDERSIDE!

WITH A *FURY* LIKE I HAVE NEVER SEEN, THE WEREWOLF TORE AT THE SPIDER.

AND SLOWLY I FOLLOWED...

THE WEREWOLF THEN BOUNDED UP THE STEPS TO THE NEXT LEVEL.

...AND DID NOT STOP TEARING UNTIL LONG AFTER THE SPIDER STOPPED MOVING AND WAS DEAD.

...TRYING NOT TO GET TOO CLOSE FOR FEAR THAT THE BEAST WOULD *CATCH MY SCENT* AND TURN AGAINST ME.

13

ABOVE ME, I COULD HEAR THE WEREWOLF BREAKING THROUGH A LARGE DOOR.

RRAAHHH!

KRUNCH

AND THEN I COULD HEAR WHAT SOUNDED LIKE MANY CREATURES, AND FLAPPING WINGS.

SKREE!

SKREE!

SKREEEE!

RROOWRR!

SKREEEEEE!

IN THE DARKNESS, I COULD NOT SEE THE CREATURES FLYING TOWARD ME UNTIL IT WAS TOO LATE!

THE WINGED THING *STRUCK* ME IN THE HEAD, AND NEARLY MADE ME *TUMBLE DOWN* THE GIANT STONE STEPS.

SWRIK!

THE CREATURE LEFT A *NASTY CUT* IN MY SCALP.

I TORE OFF A STRIP OF CLOTH FROM MY CLOAK AND BANDAGED MYSELF.

AFTER I REACHED THE NEXT FLOOR, I REALISED THAT I COULD NO LONGER HEAR THE WEREWOLF OR THE ATTACK OF THOSE WINGED MONSTERS. I COULD HEAR *NOTHING* AT ALL, EXCEPT FOR THE WIND'S HOWLING ECHO THROUGH THE BLACK TOWER.

THE SILENCE COMBINED WITH THE DARKNESS SOON BECAME TERRIFYING. I MOVED *SLOWLY* AND *SILENTLY*, NOT KNOWING WHAT I WOULD FIND IN THE HUGE EMPTY ROOM.

AND THEN, FROM NOWHERE, THE WEREWOLF STEPPED OUT OF THE SHADOWS AND STOOD RIGHT BEFORE ME.

THE BEAST WAS *STARING* INTO MY EYES. A WING FROM ONE OF THOSE CREATURES HUNG IN ITS JAWS!

I REALISED NOW THE REASON FOR THE SILENCE - THE WEREWOLF HAD DEVOURED ALL THOSE WINGED MONSTERS...

AND I FEARED THAT I WOULD BE *NEXT!*

THE WEREWOLF LEANED IN AND *STARED DOWN* UPON ME...

AND THEN THE WEREWOLF TURNED AND LEFT ME.

SNIFF!

GRMPH!

...I *FROZE* IN HORROR.

PERHAPS HIS BRUTE MIND SENSED I WAS NO THREAT, OR IT HAD SOME MEMORY OF OUR AGREEMENT WHEN IT WAS IN HUMAN FORM.

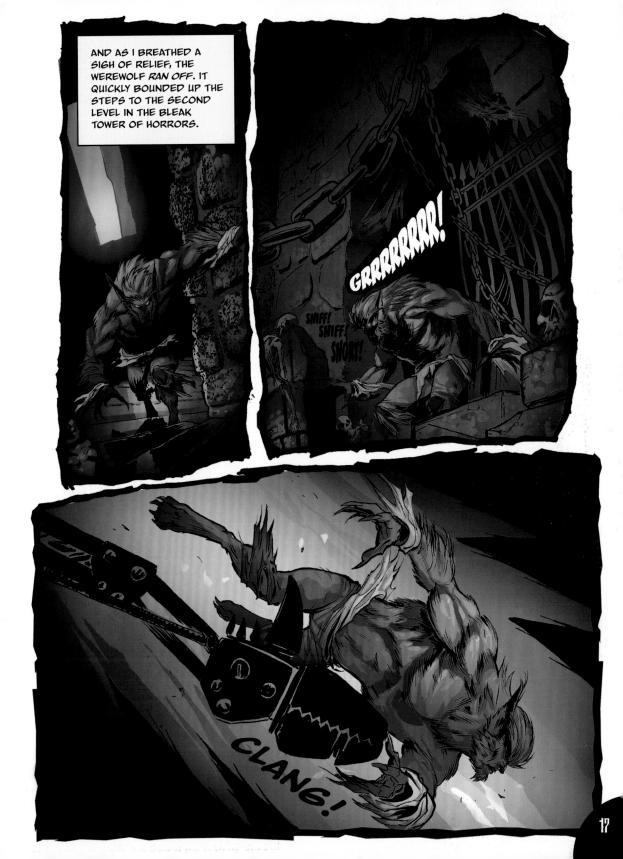

AND AS I BREATHED A SIGH OF RELIEF, THE WEREWOLF *RAN OFF*. IT QUICKLY BOUNDED UP THE STEPS TO THE SECOND LEVEL IN THE BLEAK TOWER OF HORRORS.

RRRAUGH -OACK!

I REACHED THE SECOND FLOOR AND IN THE *GLOOM* I COULD SEE THE WEREWOLF IN A VICE-LIKE MECHANICAL GRIP. IT WAS HELD BY ONE OF THE MOST FEARSOME ABOMINATIONS I HAVE EVER LAID EYES ON.

NURRR!

URRGH!

THE WEREWOLF WAS *THRASHING* LIKE A WOUNDED AND SCARED ANIMAL!

THIS SITUATION LOOKED MOST *DANGEROUS* AND *GRIM*.

I FELT IT BEST THAT I SHOULD STAY WELL OUT OF SIGHT...

...AND OUT OF HARM'S WAY.

BUT AS QUICK AS *LIGHTNING*, THE WEREWOLF *POUNCED* THROUGH THE MONSTER'S LEGS.

THE MONSTER *STUCK* ITS CLAW INTO THE STONE FLOOR!

HURFF!

THE WEREWOLF USED ITS RAZOR-LIKE CLAWS TO *CRIPPLE* THE MONSTER'S LEGS.

SLASH!!

AND AS THE TWO-HEADED MONSTER BEGAN TO FALL TO ITS KNEES, THE WEREWOLF USED A LENGTH OF CHAIN TO CHOKE IT!

HNNH!

CLINK!

ACK!

RRAUGH!

RRRAAAUUUGH!

SHKLUK

AND WITH A *FURY* TO MATCH THE MOST VIOLENT THUNDERSTORM, THE WEREWOLF *RIPPED* THE MECHANICAL CLAW FROM ITS SOCKET!

AND THEN THE WEREWOLF TURNED ITS FACE UP TOWARD THE MOON AND LET OUT A VICTORIOUS HOWL.

ITS FACE WAS A *MASK OF MADNESS.*

HOW THE WEREWOLF FINALLY DISPOSED OF THE TWO-HEADED MONSTER IS TOO GRUESOME TO TELL.

RRAUUUUGH!

AAARROOOOO!

24

HIIISSS!

BACK!! FOUL DEMON!

FATHER BASTA! HELP US!

CHILDREN!? ARE YOU ALL RIGHT?

RRRAAAUUUGH!

HRRK!

WHY DO YOU DO THIS?

CAN YOU REALLY EXPECT TO LIFT MY *CURSE* FROM YOUR LAND? I AM THE VAMPIRE MISTRESS WHO IS *WORSHIPPED* BY ALL THE NIGHT'S CREATURES!

I AM THE REASON THE NIGHT IS *CHILLED!* MY BLACK CURSE IS UNDYING!

A *FROST* UPON THE FORESTS AND MOUNTAINS THAT WILL NEVER MELT!

I HAVE HUMBLED EVEN THE GREAT *COUNT DRACULA!* MY BLACK CURSE IS UNDYING!

UPON THE FORESTS AND MOUNTAINS THAT WILL NEVER MELT! I AM THE *DESTROYER OF LIFE!*

AND YOU, *PREACHER!* MAN OF GOD! YOU WHO TURN TO THE DARKNESS FOR SALVATION!

I COULD HEAR THE BATTLE RAGING BETWEEN WANDESSA AND THE WEREWOLF. BUT MY ONLY CONCERN AT THAT MOMENT WAS GETTING THE CHILDREN OUT OF THE TOWER AND TO SAFETY.

WHY DO YOU FIGHT ME?!

CRUK -CRASH!

AND BACK AT THE ENTRANCE, I SENT THEM ON THEIR WAY.

CHILDREN RUN! DOWN THE TRAIL TO INGELSCHATT PASS.

MR. VAN RIPPER IS WAITING FOR YOU WITH A CARRIAGE TO TAKE YOU BACK HOME.

RUN!

AND DON'T LOOK BACK!

AS I SAW THE TWO CHILDREN RUN TOWARD THE WOODED PATH, I NOTICED LIGHT ON THE HORIZON.

AND AS I LOOKED ON, THE WARMTH OF *HOPE* BEGAN TO FILL MY SPIRIT.

AAIIIIEEE NO! NOT THE SUN!

AS SOON AS THE SUN'S RAYS SPREAD FROM THE TREES, WANDESSA'S WINGS BURNED TO ASH!

CRUMBLE!

THE TWO RAGING MONSTERS CAME CRASHING DOWN FROM THE ROOF OF THE TOWER.

RRRAAAUUUGH!

AUUGH!

FOOM!

NO! NO! NO! NOT LIKE THIS!

UGH! OHHHH ...OH! IT'S OVER.

BACK IN THE MAIN HALL OF THE TOWER, I MET THE NAMELESS MAN. I *THANKED* HIM FOR HELPING ME SAVE THE TWO CHILDREN AND FOR *RIDDING* US OF THE TERROR OF WANDESSA.

BUT I FELT *COLD* AND *NUMB*, FOR I KNEW WHAT WAS TO FOLLOW. AND IT TERRIFIED ME MORE THAN ANY OF THE MONSTERS I ENCOUNTERED THAT NIGHT.

FATHER BASTA, I HAVE FULFILLED MY DUTY, WE... WE HAD AN AGREEMENT. DID YOU BRING IT?

YES, IT'S HERE IN MY SATCHEL. ER, YES, PAYMENT UPON MORNING'S LIGHT, *ONE PIECE OF SILVER.*

PUH-PLEASE...

ONE SILVER BULLET THROUGH THE HEART.

BANG!

AAGH!

GAH! TH-THANK YOU FATHER!...

PUH-PRAY FOR ME FATHER...

PRAY I FIND *FINAL* AND *ETERNAL* PEACE...ACK!

PRAY I AM FORGIVEN...

AND I DID PRAY FOR HIM. THE MAN'S BODY LAY UPON *DUST* AND *DECAY*, WITH THE MOST CONTENT LOOK UPON HIS FACE.

THAT IS WHERE I LEFT HIM.

THERE IS EVIL IN THIS WORLD AND I DID WHAT MUST BE DONE TO PROTECT MY PARISH FROM THE MOST *SUPERNATURAL* OF EVILS. AND I HOPE THAT I BROUGHT *FINAL PEACE* TO A MAN WHO BRAVELY FOUGHT TO EARN SUCH PEACE.

I CAN ONLY PRAY THAT MY PEOPLE AND MY TOWN CAN NOW AWAKE TO THE LIGHT OF A BRIGHTER FUTURE.

This edition first published in 2010 by
Franklin Watts
338 Euston Road
London NW1 3BH

Franklin Watts Australia
Level 17/207 Kent Street
Sydney NSW 2000

First published in the USA by Magic Wagon, a division of the ABDO Group

1 3 5 7 9 10 8 6 4 2

Written and illustrated by Jeff Zornow
Letters and colours by Jay Fotos
Edited and directed by Chazz DeMoss
Cover design by Neil Klinepier
UK cover design by Peter Scoulding

A CIP catalogue record for this book is available from the British Library.

Dewey number: 741.5

ISBN: 978 0 7496 9685 6

Printed in China

Franklin Watts is a division of Hachette Children's Books,
an Hachette UK company.
www.hachette.co.uk

READ THE REST OF THIS STORY IN: MUMMY